Sketching Outdoors in Spring

Crocus sprouts
from low angle
April 4 '86

Sketching Outdoors in Spring

Crocuses in bloom
April '86

BY JIM ARNOSKY

LOTHROP, LEE & SHEPARD BOOKS   NEW YORK

This season is dedicated to

L O U I S   P O R T E R

First Edition   1 2 3 4 5 6 7 8 9 10

10/87

Library of Congress Cataloging in Publication Data   Arnosky, Jim.   Sketching outdoors in spring. Summary:
Provides drawings of landscapes, plants, animals, and other aspects of nature, accompanied by comments from
the artist on how and why he drew them. 1. Outdoor life in art—Juvenile literature. 2. Animals in art—
Juvenile literature. 3. Plants in art—Juvenile literature. 4. Wildlife art—Juvenile literature. 5. Landscape in
art—Juvenile literature. 6. Spring in art—Juvenile literature. 7. Drawing—Technique—Juvenile literature.
[1. Nature (Aesthetics) 2. Landscape drawing—Technique. 3. Animal painting and illustration—Technique.
4. Drawing—Technique] I. Title. NC825.O88A76   1987   743'.83   86-21308   ISBN 0-688-06284-9

And this our life, exempt from public haunt,
Finds tongues in trees, books in the running brooks,
Sermons in stones, and good in everything.

WILLIAM SHAKESPEARE
As You Like It

Male catkins of a
Pussy willow
drawn in sleet and snow
April 6 1986

INTRODUCTION

The pictures in this book were drawn from life during one season—spring. Some were sketched in a flash. Others, more detailed, were made when I could sit and look and carefully draw what I was seeing. All the pictures on these pages have been reproduced actual size so you can see them exactly the way they looked to me as I sketched them. As I drew, thoughts occurred to me about the nature of the seasonable subjects I had chosen and ways to capture them on paper. These "drawing thoughts" are included, set apart from the main text.

All of my sketching is done using a minimum of art supplies. In one shirt pocket I carry two soft-leaded pencils, a small sharpener, and one kneadable eraser. These things, along with a pad of quality drawing paper, make up my necessities.

As comforts I bring along a small folding stool to sit on and a pair of polarized sunglasses to cut the sun's glare off the white paper. When drawing outdoor scenes, I employ a portable wooden easel.

I work outdoors in all weather. In the early days of spring, when it is still quite wintry, I wear warm woolen gloves. I also use an umbrella to sketch under when it is raining. Because of my special interest in wildlife, I always keep a pair of binoculars handy.

To each and every artist I recommend spending some time each season sketching outdoors. You will find working in the open air refreshing. Weather, fair or foul, somehow invigorates your drawing lines. And each day afield you will produce pictures that you might not otherwise have imagined.

Jim Arnosky
Ramtails
Spring 1986

I BEGAN MY SPRING DRAWINGS IN MARCH, when in many places deep snow still lay upon the ground. On one raw and snowy day, sketching with woolen gloves on, I did this drawing of my neighbor's sugarhouse. Inside, where it was warm, my neighbor was boiling maple sap that he had collected from his tapped trees. The water being boiled out of the sap rose as vapor that escaped through the little house's open roof, creating a small, sweetly scented cloud in the wintry woods.

When drawing buildings or other man-made objects on the spot, don't overly concern yourself with making lines that are straight and true. Capture the feeling of the place around the structure— the land, the vegetation, the air and sky. There will be plenty of time later at home to level your building's horizontal lines and straighten any vertical lines that may be terribly off plumb.

In cold weather, when sketching with gloved hands, I keep my pencil less than sharp. The combination of a dull point and soft lead makes it possible to draw good substantial lines quickly.

9

Deep in the maple woods I found this broken tree. It had been rotting for years and had finally succumbed to winter wind and snow. The whiteness of the wood inside the huge stump showed the break was recent. Two maple saplings that had been growing in the shade of the giant old tree are now standing in the light.

A leaf-littered woodland floor can be suggested by a scribbling of leafy shapes and shadows.

It is easier to apply shading when your pencil point is dull.

To draw the darkened place inside the hollow tree trunk, I lightly outlined the area, then added the shading. Afterward I drew in the darker lines of texture and details.

When amid broken and fallen trees, be careful to stay safely away from any other potential deadfalls.

Broken Maple
JEA 1986

In the springtime woods you will find many dead tree trunks and individual branches that have been broken and blown down by winter storms. Each and every piece is interesting to look at and to draw. I spent one entire afternoon high atop a mountain, lost in the intricate details of this windfall. As I sketched, a woodpecker began hammering somewhere in the distance. It was chipping away at another dead but not yet fallen branch.

Woodland is so visually exciting, it can overwhelm you. Whenever you feel overwhelmed by a scene, pick one thing in it that interests you—a single tree, a fallen branch, or even a boulder—and begin drawing that.

Sometimes, after you begin a drawing, your subject will seem less interesting on paper than it appears in reality. You may be drawing it too small. You may simply be seeing it too small. Move closer to it.

Fallen branches near Kettle Pond
Jim Arnosky April 1986

13

In spring, streams fill with melting snow and ice, rise up over their banks, and flood the surrounding land. Every little brook becomes a torrent. I sketched this mountain brook on three different days in April, when snow from the high country was still melting into it.

The first day the water was so high I couldn't see the stream bed at all. The rushing stream cascaded over rock ledges, creating white-capped waves, and washed up onto the boulder-strewn land high above its banks.

To sketch a fast-moving stream, you really have to loosen up. Draw rapidly, always making your lines in the same direction as the flow.

The sound of the rushing water should set your drawing rhythm.

A lively stream can be intimidating when you begin sketching it. Watch the flow and you will notice that the moving water repeats the same simple patterns over and over. Ripples ripple. Swirls keep swirling. Plunges, spills, slaps, and splashes are performed continuously. Each stream wave is a recreation of one preceding it.

water spilling over a ledge
April 13 '86

The second day I set my easel near a place where various logs, branches, and building boards that had been carried downstream by the flood formed a jam against two sturdy birches. The birch trees are part of a rocky midstream island.

High water flotsam
April 14, 1986

17

Soon after all the snow had gone from the mountains, the volume of water in the brook diminished. The water level lowered and the noise of the running stream quieted. Surfaces of pools calmed and I could see down to their sandy bottoms once again. All the while I sketched this lovely little pool, I expected to see the liquid form of a trout moving in the dark water.

In a rushing stream the dark water indicates the general flow. The white water shows where the stream leaps, tumbles, pauses, or veers away from the main flow.

Work on each waterfall until it is clear how much water is pouring, what it is going over, and where it is spilling to.

Notice that the streamside boulders look dry and the rock in the falls looks wet.

Once you have your water scene drawn, go over the picture once more, adding a dark line here or a bit of shading there to help distinguish water from rock.

Every boulder has a number of surfaces. Each surface is a different rock face, with its own marks, scars, clefts, and fissures. The longer you look at a boulder, the more of its individual history you will perceive.

A stream run, some bank boulders, and a small side falls
JEH April 15 1986

Trees growing close to water are apt to have roots showing above the surface of the ground. In early spring, with the snow cover gone and no greenery to obscure them, such roots are exposed models of strenuous living.

Over time the roots of a tree can wrap around a large boulder and crack it into smaller pieces. Often these same roots hold the broken mass together.

Yellow birch growing right beside stream
April '86

Hemlock root near lake shore

Rucker's pond (outflowing stream)
Spotting rain and snow —
Married roots of hemlock & birch
growing around rock
April '86

I sketched this herculean shoreline pine on the first truly warm day of spring. It is the first spring drawing that I did without having to wear winter gloves. The sun was as bright as it was warm. Light played all over the massive roots and clearly defined each stratum of the ledge the tree stands upon.

The longer I sit drawing a root dug into the ground or a boulder embedded in the earth, the more I feel I too am becoming rooted to my spot.

After three hours spent sitting before this great tree and thinking of its growth, I had to pry myself from my seat when it was time to leave.

Any drawing done outdoors will seem incomplete when you are forced by aching muscles, hunger, or fading light to pack up and go home. Back home, however, away from the reality of your subject and its surrounding scenery, your picture will look finished and full of interesting details.

Shore Pine

Male Woodfrogs
— Bob Hines 18 1956

In a soggy April woods I heard the clucking calls of male wood
frogs. I followed the sounds to a small spring pool and found
three males competing vocally to attract a mate. By getting down
on my belly and pulling myself toward them, I was able to get
close enough to see not only the frogs' heads sticking up out of
the water but also their bodies hanging suspended under the
water's surface.

*When suddenly discovered, wild animals often will freeze in
their position and stay motionless for as long as they feel they
are being watched.*

*Whenever I can, I draw things their actual size. This gives an
added measure of information to my pictures.*

*All of the fiddleheads in a cluster emanate from nearly the same
spot of earth. When you draw fiddelheads, show this, and show
that each individual fiddlehead is facing a different direction.
This way they have of "looking about" in all directions is what
gives fiddleheads their charm.*

The calling of the frogs signaled the coming of fiddleheads. I began seeing fuzzy clusters of them everywhere in the woods, on the banks of streams and shores of ponds, and along the edges of fields. Most were sprouting green from the composted mounds of previous years' fern growth. Some fiddleheads were sprouting in new places—fresh, festive-looking newcomers pushing up through the leaf mold.

Fiddleheads – all drawn actual size
JEA April 86

The first wildflowers of spring are loners that grow in secluded, often hard-to-get-at spots. Drawing them from life can mean going on safari and sketching in some uncomfortable places.

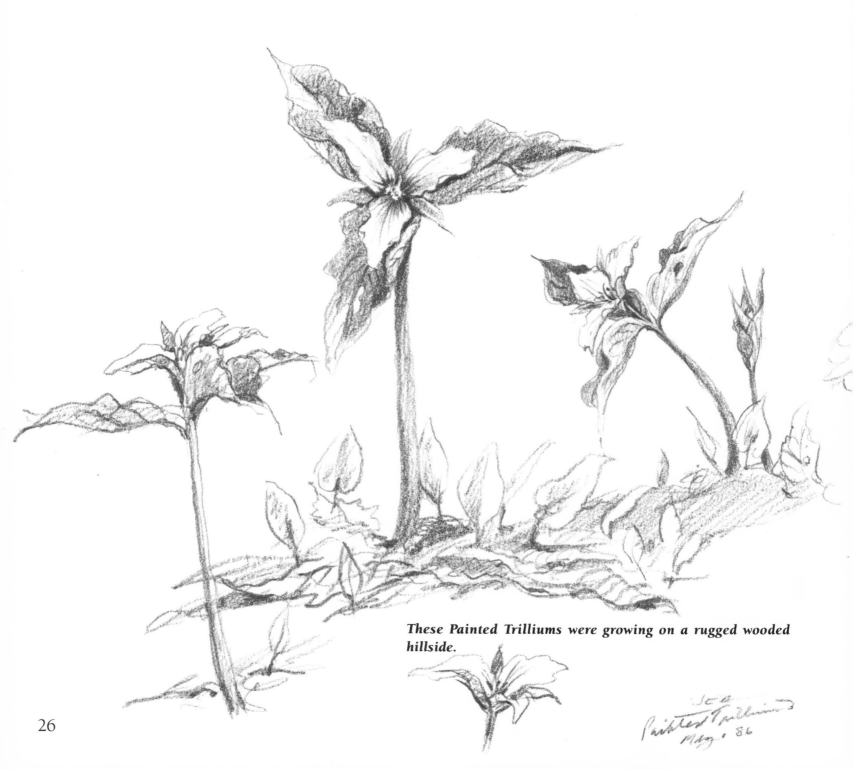

These Painted Trilliums were growing on a rugged wooded hillside.

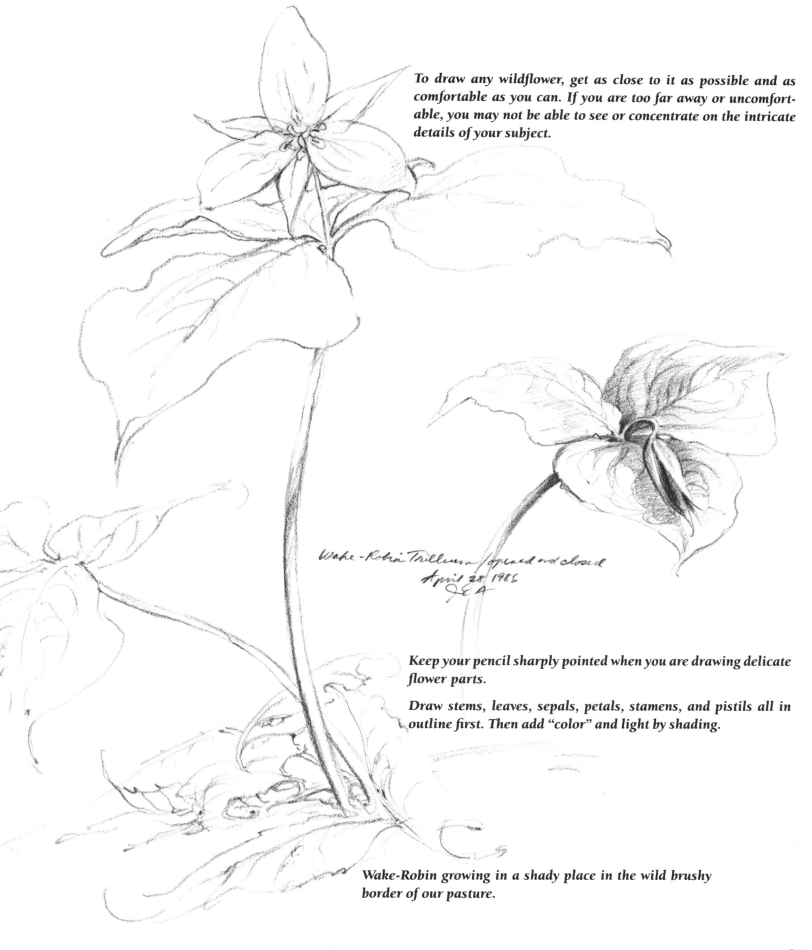

To draw any wildflower, get as close to it as possible and as comfortable as you can. If you are too far away or uncomfortable, you may not be able to see or concentrate on the intricate details of your subject.

Wake-Robin Trillium (opened and closed)
April 28 1985
JEA

Keep your pencil sharply pointed when you are drawing delicate flower parts.

Draw stems, leaves, sepals, petals, stamens, and pistils all in outline first. Then add "color" and light by shading.

Wake-Robin growing in a shady place in the wild brushy border of our pasture.

Trout Lilies –
front / side / back
April 30 1986

**Trout Lilies flourishing on the sun-dappled banks of a
small brook.**

I made this sketch just after a warm rain. In the damp shady woods where these Moccasin Flowers thrive, mosquitos were out in squadrons. Repellent, long sleeves, and even my mesh head net could not protect me from them. I came home bitten and itching.

Moccasin Flowers are also known as Pink Lady's Slippers.

29

Wherever you discover wildflowers just beginning to grow, revisit the place often to see how they develop. Here are periodic sketches I made of a Jack-in-the-Pulpit, from the moment I first noticed its pointed nose sticking up out of the soil to the day it stood fully formed.

In drawing, color and markings are suggested with shades of gray, from pale and nearly white to rich and deep tones that range toward solid black. Learn to vary and control your hand pressure when you are drawing and you will be able to achieve this spectrum of grays with one soft-leaded pencil.

Colors are most vivid in the clear light of rain-washed air. After a rain I like to roam, sketchbook in hand, knowing something lovely will catch my eye.

I sketched the final stage of this Jack-in-the-Pulpit during one of our rainiest weeks. Notice how brilliant it looks.

The Jack-in-the-Pulpit is a solitary flower that grows in moist woods.

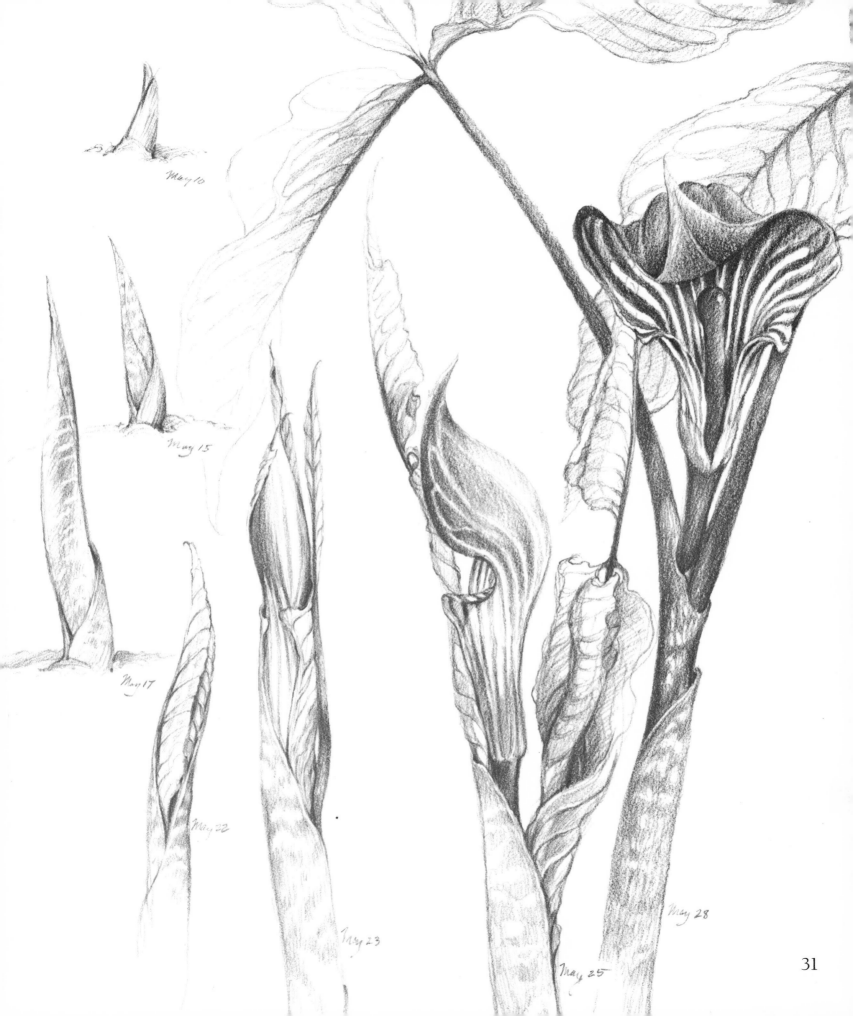

May 10

May 15

May 17

May 22

May 23

May 25

May 28

Springtime scenes are open and airy-looking. Here a fisherman, anticipating the coming season, has cached his boat on the shore of the pond. Now it looks obvious, but as the foliage grows in around it, the boat will gradually become hidden and will eventually be invisible to passersby.

With this sketch I learned not to judge a picture while it is still in the works. Twice I had nearly convinced myself to quit drawing this scene. Once because the boat, from the angle at which I was seeing it, proved difficult to draw. Again when a heavy bank of clouds blocked the sun, and the light that gave shape to my drawing was lost. The sunlight returned. I mastered the subtle shape of the boat and came out of the forest with one of the finest pictures I had made all spring.

Boat cached along the shore
of Kettle Pond
May 1 '86

While I was drawing the fisherman's boat, I spotted a loon swimming out in the pond. Using binoculars, I made two quick sketches. The first was a side view of the loon's head, neck, and back. The second was drawn even more rapidly just after the bird had emerged from a dive with a small fish in its bill.

I drew only what I saw, and from that distance, even with the aid of binoculars, I could not see the loon's eyes or nostrils. I could make out only a spattering of its bold black-and-white markings. As I was drawing my last lines, the loon dived again. This time, underwater, it swam away.

Sometimes a quick glimpse of an animal with your naked eyes is vision enough to recall and draw what you saw. The way this white-throated sparrow was perched with up-cocked tail left enough of an impression in my mind that, after the bird had flown, I was able to make this sketch.

Blackbirds sketched from
the recollection of a quick glimpse
May 5 '86

When the impulse strikes you to draw from life, however fleeting the opportunity, do so! Any one of these rough springtime sketches, all drawn hastily, can later be used as the basis for a more detailed and finished picture. Some days your quickest sketches will be your best work.

Reptiles and large birds can move so slowly they appear to be holding a pose for you.

Snapper *draws quickly as seen through binoculars*

Quick studies of animals you are seeing through binoculars often show a high level of accuracy in capturing moods, poses, and actions. This may be because the looking we do through binoculars is an intense type of seeing.

Sundown 50 yards woodchuck at May 1 1986

During a gentle spring rain small birds remain active, but they perch more often to rest, dry off, and preen their feathers. Sketch each perched pose for as long as the bird holds it.

This sketch was done on a blustery May afternoon. I was attracted to the scene by the contrast between the sturdy stone wall and the slender poplar trees that were being whipped about by the wind. Some gusts were so strong they threatened to take my easel with them. No matter how strong the wind, the poplars' tiny spring leaves held fast to their branches.

Some trees and shrubs leaf out in early spring. Others develop leaves later in the season. Let your spring sketches reflect this variety by showing which trees already have leaves and which trees are still in bud.

Small springtime leaves seen from a distance appear as dots, dashes, ovals, and arrowheads. These are also the shapes used in drawings to suggest spring leaves.

Stonewall & poplars
on a very windy day
J.E.A. May 1986

39

While resting streamside during a long day of fishing, I noticed this male smallmouth bass. He was in shallow water, guarding a circular nest he had cleared away in the gravelly bottom.

The fish was immediately aware of me, but he stayed over his nest even after I had approached to within three feet. All the while I sketched, the bass appeared not to be threatened. His fins and tail waved serenely in the water.

I presumed that one or more females had already deposited eggs in the nest and that the eggs were there, hidden among the glistening pebbles and sand granules. Papa smallmouth himself blended so well with the water color and the stream bottom that even with my polarized glasses on I more than once lost sight of him.

JEA
Smallmouth on nest
White River —
May 86

Mallard on her nest
Jean May 6 1986

The female mallard was on her nest when I first saw her. I was close enough to see her in lovely detail but still far enough away so as not to frighten her off her eggs. I didn't press that luck and stayed only as long as necessary to get most of this picture completed. Later, well away from the nest site, I added the finishing touches.

One morning I spotted the male mallard standing on the pond shore, asleep. I was able to sneak to within eight feet of him and began making this sketch. Suddenly the duck awoke, spread the feathers of one wing in a lazy stretch, and walked away.

Male
Mallard Jean May 8 1986

The next time I visited the mallard hen, she was becoming a mother. I found myself sketching frantically to keep up with her active brood.

Ducklings were still hatching, out of sight under their mother's broad feathery form. Those that had already emerged were quacking softly all around her. Soon they were investigating the ground. Any sudden movement or loud noise sent them all scurrying back to Mama where, pressed against her flanks, they felt safe.

Ducks Unlimited May 10 1986 / May 11 Mother's Day!

I like to get down low near ground level to draw tiny animals such as these ducklings.

43

Domestic animals, though wary initially, quickly become accustomed to strangers. When I first approached their pen, these piglets stood stock still. Each pair of beady eyes was sizing me up. Once I began my sketching, they forgot about me and began to behave naturally.

If an animal you are sketching suddenly moves (as is likely to happen), keep drawing the pose it had for as long as you can recall it. Then wait, adding a few more lines each time your subject approximates the original position.

Keep on drawing even if your first attempts are obviously bad. With each completed figure you will have learned more about your subject's anatomy. Your lines will become more sure, your sketches more accurate.

Every time I draw animals from life, I see a marked improvement in my figures from the first to the last sketch in a series.

Mr. Welsh's piglets
Jan — May 1986
cold / blustery

Sheep resting
Wm Amory
Mayo

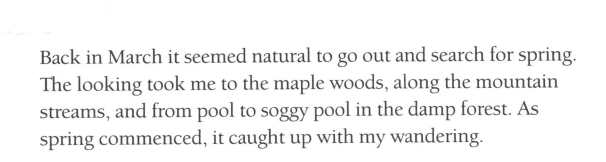

When drawing from life scenes that feature animals, begin with a light horizon line to give your picture a plane on which to appear. Quickly block in the animals, starting with those which are standing still. Sketch others that are moving about. Then concentrate on the scenery around the figures. Once you have the entire scene sketched in, add light by applying shadows.

The three-dimensional shape and musculature of an animal are both easier to see and easier to draw when the animal is molded by light and shadow. If you find you are having trouble constructing a particular animal, perhaps you should wait until you can see it in brighter light. Then try drawing it again.

Back in March it seemed natural to go out and search for spring. The looking took me to the maple woods, along the mountain streams, and from pool to soggy pool in the damp forest. As spring commenced, it caught up with my wandering.

Soon I didn't have to go far to do my springtime sketching. Here, my wife, Deanna, is busy doing her spring planting in soil I tilled. In the next few weeks, when new plants grow from the seeds she sows, spring will have become summer.